Today Tomorrow & Always

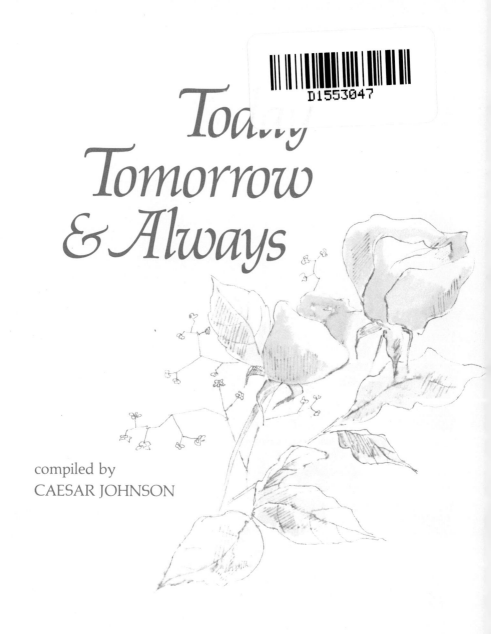

compiled by
CAESAR JOHNSON

THE C. R. GIBSON COMPANY, NORWALK, CONNECTICUT

CONTENTS

I

A RAIN OF DIAMONDS

Love is
   a rain of diamonds
   in the mind

   the soul's fruit
   sliced in two

   a dark spring
   loosed at the lips of light

   under-earth waters
   unlocked from their lurking
   to sparkle in a crevice
   parted by the sun

   a temple
   not of stone but cloud

   beyond the heart's roar
   and all violence

   outside the anvil-stunned domain
   unfrenzied space

   between the grains of change
   blue permanence

   one short step
   to the good ground

   the bite into bread again

                    May Swenson

When two individuals meet, so do two private worlds. None
of our private worlds is big enough for us to live a
wholesome life in. We need the wider world of joy and
wonder, of purpose and venture, of toil and tears. What are
we, any of us, but strangers and sojourners forlornly
wandering through the nighttime until we draw together
and find the meaning of our lives in one another, dissolving
our fears in each other's courage, making music together
and lighting torches to guide us through the dark? We
belong together. Love is what we need. To love and to be
loved. Let our hearts be open; and what we would receive
from others, let us give. For what is given still remains to
bless the giver—when the gift is love.

A. Powell Davis

DESTINY

Somewhere there waiteth in this world of ours
For one lone soul another lonely soul,
Each choosing each through all the weary hours
And meeting strangely at one sudden goal.
Then blend they, like green leaves with golden flowers,
Into one beautiful and perfect whole;
And life's long night is ended, and the way
Lies open onward to eternal day.

Edwin Arnold

The more you love, the more love you are given to love with.

Lucien Price

7

Mutual love is the only basis of a human relationship; and bargains and claims and promises are attempts to substitute something else; and they introduce falsity into the relationship. No human being can have rights in another, and no human being can grant to another rights in himself or herself.

If you love a person you love him or her in their stark reality, and refuse to shut your eyes to their defects and errors. For to do that is to shut your eyes to their needs. Love cannot abide deceit, or pretense or unreality. It rests only in the reality of the loved one, demands that the loved one should be himself, so that it may love him for himself.

John MacMurray

DEBT

My debt to you, Belovèd,
  Is one I cannot pay
In any coin of any realm
  On any reckoning day;

For where is he shall figure
  The debt, when all is said,
To one who makes you dream again
  When all the dreams were dead?

Or where is the appraiser
  Who shall the claim compute
Of one who makes you sing again
  When all the songs were mute?

Jessie B. Rittenhouse

WHY DO I LOVE YOU?

Is it the blue eyes or the green sweater?

Is it the soaring intellect or that she dusts like your mother?

Most of us do not really know why we love the people we do, but one woman was able to verbalize her feelings. She is a successful woman who has had her successes with men, too, and for years she has been faithful to just one man. Why?

"Because," she said, "he loves me. He loves me even though he has seen me at my worst, at times when I don't really deserve to be loved. He has loved me then. And he has loved me at good times, too." Then she paused and said, "I suppose that sounds very selfish."

What most of us fail to realize is that love is not all giving, and if we are honest with ourselves and those we love, we plan to take, too. We want to take. We need to take. And although we look for a lot of worldly reasons to love another, one of the strongest reasons for love is that we are loved.

Do you love somebody enough to be loved in return?

John Mack Carter and Lois Wyse

Kindness in words creates confidence,
kindness in thinking creates profoundness,
kindness in giving creates love.

Lao-Tse

Love, though proverbially blind, is often very prone to see something which has no existence whatever.

E. F. Benson

Shine! shine! shine!
Pour down your warmth, great sun!
While we bask, we two together.

Two together!
Winds blow south, or winds blow north,
Day come white, or night come black,
Home, or rivers and mountains from home,
Singing all time, minding no time,
While we two keep together.

Walt Whitman

Love is the emblem of eternity: it confounds all notion of time: effaces all memory of a beginning, all fear of an end.

Madame de Staël

If you wish women to love you, be original; I know a man who used to wear felt boots summer and winter, and women fell in love with him.

Anton Chekhov

Love consists in this
that two solitudes protect and
touch and greet each other.

Rainer Maria Rilke

This is the miracle that happens every time to those who really love: the more they give, the more they possess of that precious nourishing love from which flowers and children have their strength and which could help all human beings if they would take it without doubting . . .

Rainer Maria Rilke

Madam, it is the hardest thing in the world to be in love, and yet attend to business. A gentleman asked me this morning, "What news from Lisbon?" and I answered, "She is exquisitely handsome."

Sir Richard Steele

Love is always building up. It puts some line of beauty on every life it touches. It gives new hope to discouraged ones, new strength to those who are weak, new joys to those who are sorrowing. It makes life seem more worthwhile to every one into whose eyes it looks.

Anonymous

THINGS LOVELIER

You cannot dream
Things lovelier
Than the first love
I had of her.

Nor air is any
By magic shaken
As her first breath in
The first kiss taken.

And who, in dreaming,
Understands
Her hands stretched like
A blind man's hands?

Open, trembling,
Wise, they were—
You cannot dream
Things lovelier.

Humbert Wolfe

Love withers under constraint: its very essence is liberty: it
is compatible neither with obedience, jealousy, nor fear.

Percy Bysshe Shelley

For me to love is to commit myself, freely and without reservation. I am sincerely interested in your happiness and well-being. Whatever your needs are, I will try to fulfill them. If you are lonely and need me, I will talk. If you need the strength of human touch, I will touch you. If you need to be held, I will hold you.

I will try to be constant with you so that you will understand the core of my personality and from that understanding you can gain strength and security that I am acting as me. I want to become a truly loving person. Knowing you has opened me to a new and different understanding of what a loving attitude and way of life can mean. It is my hope that our lives may be a continual renewal of our love for one another and for other people.

Walter Rinder

SONNET III

I would not have this perfect love of ours
Grow from a single root, a single stem,
Bearing no goodly fruit, but only flowers
That idly hide life's iron diadem:
It should grow always like that Eastern tree
Whose limbs take root and spread forth constantly;
That love for one, from which there doth not spring
Wide love for all, is but a worthless thing.
Not in another world, as poets prate,
Dwell we apart above the tide of things,
High floating o'er earth's clouds on faery wings;
But our pure love doth ever elevate
Into a holy bond of brotherhood
All earthly things, making them pure and good.

James Russell Lowell

That there should exist one other person in the world toward whom all openness of exchange should establish itself, from whom there should be no concealment, whose body should be as dear to one, in every part as one's own; with whom there should be no sense of mine or thine, in property or possession; into whose mind one's thoughts should naturally flow, as it were; to know whom and oneself, there should be a spontaneous rebound of sympathy in all the joys and sorrows and experiences of life; such is perhaps one of the dearest wishes of the soul.

Edward Carpenter

Doubt of the reality of love ends by making us doubt everything.

Frédéric Amiel

THE HUMAN TOUCH

'Tis the human touch in this world that counts,
The touch of your hand and mine,
Which means far more to the fainting heart
Than shelter and bread and wine;
For shelter is gone when the night is o'er,
And bread lasts only a day,
But the touch of the hand and the sound of the voice
Sing on in the soul alway.

Spencer Michael Free

THE GROWTH OF LOVE

Love that I know, love I am wise in, love,
My strength, my pride, my grace, my skill untaught,
My faith here upon earth, my hope above,
My contemplation and perpetual thought:
The pleasure of my fancy, my heart's fire,
My joy, my peace, my praise, my happy theme,
The aim of all my doing, my desire
Of being, my life by day, by night my dream:

Love, my sweet melancholy, my distress,
My pain, my doubt, my trouble, my despair,
My only folly and unhappiness,
And in my careless moments still my care:
O love, sweet love, earthly love, love divine,
Say'st thou today, O love, that thou art mine?

Robert Bridges

*The reduction of the universe to a simple being,
the expansion of a single being even to God,
this is love.*

Victor Hugo

II

WEDDING DAY

WEDDING SONG

And my smile will know your joy, my love
And my eyes will know your tears.
And your name through my heart will throb,
And your life through my years.
And my lips will know your song, my love,
And your hands will know my fire,
And my need in your strength will dwell,
And my sleep within your sigh.
And my pain will know your secrets
And my trust will know your plan.
And your silence fill my empty hours,
And my heart will understand.

Buffy Sainte-Marie

Before marriage man hovers above life, observes it from
without; only in marriage does he plunge into it, entering it
through the personality of another.

Alexander Yelchaninov

*To wed is to bring not only our worldly goods but every
potential capacity to create more values in living together. . . .
In becoming one these two create a new world
that had never existed before.*

Paul E. Johnson

A happy marriage is a new beginning of life,
a new starting point for happiness and usefulness.

Arthur Penrhyn Stanley

Out of the wild exuberance of creation throughout millions
of years, you two have appeared . . . each of you unique,
distinctive, wonderously personal. You have chosen to
journey together down this earth valley in the brief moment
of time that is yours. From this day forward, you become a
unit of life that will bring forth futures. You are both called
into a new existence. The old things have passed away; a
new heaven and a new earth is now your dwelling place.
For the whole universe has come to each of you in the form
of a particular person who has a unique love for you and is
beloved by you.

Ross Snyder

We were alone, and God has given us each a beloved
companion. Long, long, and always brightening years of
thorough trust and love, dearer than was ever dreamed, lie
before us. How happy we shall be in our glowing hopes!
how happy in our generous ambitions! how happy in our
earnest life! Ah, my love! how can I love you enough for the
gift of this beautiful moment, for the promise of the fairer
times to come!

Theodore Winthrop

Marriage is the only known example of the happy meeting of the immovable object and the irresistible force.

Ogden Nash

We should marry to please ourselves, not other people.

Isaac Bickerstaffe

Marriage is our last, best chance to grow up.

Joseph Barth

A wedding:
Same old slippers,
Same old rice,
Same old glimpse of
Paradise.

William J. Lampton

. . . When you have married your wife, you would think you were got upon a hill-top, and might begin to go downward by an easy slope. But you have only ended courting to begin marriage. Falling in love and winning love are often difficult tasks to overbearing and rebellious spirits; but to keep in love is also a business of some importance, to which both man and wife must bring kindness and good will. The true love-story commences at the altar, when there lies before the married pair a most beautiful contest of wisdom and generosity, and a life-long struggle towards an unattainable ideal, ay, surely unattainable, from the very fact that they are two instead of one.—

Robert Louis Stevenson

You are about to enter into a union which is most sacred and most serious, requiring of those who enter into it a complete and unreserved giving of self. It will bind you together for life in a relationship so close and so intimate that it will profoundly affect your whole future.

That future, with its hopes and disappointments, its successes and its failures, its pleasures and its pains, its joys and its sorrows, is hidden from your eyes.

Love can make it easy, and perfect love can make it a joy. May, then, this love with which you join your hands and hearts today never fail, but grow deeper and stronger as the years go on.

From Exhortation Before Marriage

Life is not so sinister-grave.
Matter of fact has made them brave.
He is husband, she is wife.
She fears not him, they fear not life.

Robert Frost

Marriage is to share the bitter-sweet of life.

George Crabbe

Marriage is a deliberate act of will, and from this union of souls by God's decree, a sacred and inviolable bond arises.

Pope Pius XI

Two persons who have chosen each other out of all the species, with the design to be each other's mutual comfort and entertainment, have, in that action, bound themselves to be good-humored, affable, discreet, forgiving, patient, and joyful, with respect to each other's frailities and perfections, to the end of their lives.

Joseph Addison

LEST THOU FORGET

Lest thou forget in the years between
The beautiful things thine eyes have seen:
The light of the sun and the silver sheen
Of cobwebs over a field of green ...

The birth of love on a destined day
When blossomed the first sweet flowers of May
And sunlight flooded the wistful way;

The vows we took and the prayers we said
When the urge of love to the altars led
And the mystical marriage rites were read;

The sacrament scenes of death and birth;
The tragedies testing human worth—
These are the timeless things of earth!

Reverence, worship, and love and prayer,
Kneeling alone at the altar stair,
Hearing the Infinite whisper there.

William L. Stidger

Hundreds of birds in the air
And millions of leaves on the pavement.
Then the bells pealing on
Over palace and people outside,
All for the words "I will"
To love's most holy enslavement.
What can we do but rejoice
With a triumphing bridegroom
and bride?

*Sir John Betjeman, Poet Laureate (written on the occasion of the
marriage of Princess Anne to Captain Mark Phillips.)*

Between us a new morning
Is being born from our flesh
Just the right way
To put everything into shape
We are moving just the right footsteps ahead
And the earth says hello to us
The day has all our rainbows
The fireplace is lit with our eyes
And the ocean celebrates our marriage

Paul Eluard

Marriage is something you have to give your whole mind to.

Henrik Ibsen

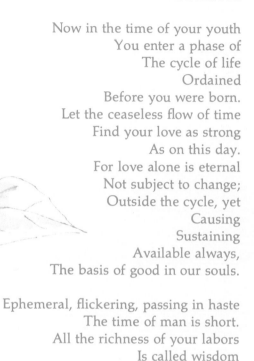

MARRIAGE

Now in the time of your youth
You enter a phase of
The cycle of life
Ordained
Before you were born.
Let the ceaseless flow of time
Find your love as strong
As on this day.
For love alone is eternal
Not subject to change;
Outside the cycle, yet
Causing
Sustaining
Available always,
The basis of good in our souls.

Ephemeral, flickering, passing in haste
The time of man is short.
All the richness of your labors
Is called wisdom
And the essence of wisdom is love.

James Lawson

One should not marry to find happiness,
but to share happiness.

Harry Emerson Fosdick

It is for the union of you and me
that there is light in the sky.
It is for the union of you and me
that the earth is decked in dusky green.

It is for the union of you and me
that night sits motionless with the world in her arms;
dawn appears opening the eastern door
with sweet murmurs in her voice.

The boat of hope sails along on the currents of
eternity towards that union,
flowers of the ages are being gathered together
for its welcoming ritual.

It is for the union of you and me
that this heart of mine, in the garb of a bride,
has proceeded from birth to birth
upon the surface of this ever-turning world
to choose the Beloved.

Rabindranath Tagore

Marriage is a mistake of youth—which we should all make.

Don Herold

Love does not consist in gazing at each other but in looking
outward together in the same direction. There is no
comradeship except through union in the same high effort.

Antoine de Saint-Exupéry

Holy is the wife; revered the mother; galliptious is the
summer girl—but the bride is the certified check among the
wedding presents that the gods send in when man is
married to mortality.

O. Henry

Marriage is a vow to please one another.

Stanislaus

III

WEALTH IS
THE VISION SHARED

I have never been rich before,
But you have poured
Into my heart's high door
A golden hoard.

My wealth is the vision shared,
The sympathy,
The feast of the soul prepared
By you for me.

Together we wander through
The wooded ways.
Old beauties are green and new
Seen through your gaze.

I look for no greater prize
Than your soft voice.
The steadiness of your eyes
Is my heart's choice.

I have never been rich before,
But I divine
Your step on my sunlit floor
And wealth is mine!

Anne Campbell

Marriage is an opportunity for happiness, not a gift. It is a
step by which two imperfect individuals unite their forces
in the struggle for happiness.

Henry C. Link

ANY HUSBAND OR WIFE

Let us be guests in one another's house
With deferential "no" and courteous "yes";
Let us take care to hide our foolish moods
Behind a certain show of cheerfulness.

Let us avoid all sullen silences;
We should find fresh and sprightly things to say;
I must be fearful lest you find me dull,
And you must dread to bore me anyway.

Let us knock gently at each other's heart,
Glad of a chance to look within—and yet,
Let us remember that to force one's way
Is the unpardoned breach of etiquette.

So, shall I be host—you, the hostess,
Until all need for entertainment ends;
We shall be lovers when the last door shuts,
But what is better still—we shall be friends.

Carol Haynes

Whatever woman may cast her lot with mine, should any
ever do so, it is my intention to do all in my power to make
her happy and contented; and there is nothing I can imagine
that would make me more unhappy than to fail in the
effort.

Abraham Lincoln

A COUPLE

He was in Cincinnati, she in Burlington.
He was in a gang of Postal Telegraph linemen.
She was a pot rassler in a boarding house.
"The crying is lonely," she wrote him.
"The same here," he answered.
The winter went by, and he came back, and they married.
And he went away again where rainstorms knocked down
telegraph poles,
And wires dropped with frozen sleet.
And again she wrote him, "the crying is lonely."
And again he answered, "the same here."
Their five children are in the public schools.
He votes the Republican ticket, and is a taxpayer.
They are known among those who know them
As honest American citizens living honest lives.
Many things that bother other people never bother them.
They have their five children, and they are a couple,
A pair of birds that call to each other and satisfy.

As sure as he goes away she writes him, "the crying is
lonely."
And he flashes back the old answer, "the same here."
It is a long time since he was a gang lineman at Cincinnati,
And she was a pot rassler in a Burlington boarding house.
Yet they never get tired of each other. They are a couple.

Carl Sandburg

All that a husband or wife really wants is to be pitied a little, praised a little, appreciated a little; and for each to realize that the hard work is not all on one side.

Warren H. Goldsmith

A WORD TO HUSBANDS

To keep your marriage brimming,
With love in the loving cup,
Whenever you're wrong, admit it;
Whenever you're right, shut up.

Ogden Nash

We have come together to make a marriage of our love and understanding. We shall share with each other in all gladness, strengthen each other in all labor, minister to each other in all sorrow, and be one with each other in the memories of life:

We shall make a home of the place where we dwell and there we shall gather wisdom from the seasons of life. It shall be a place for the gladness of children and for the joy of youth. In it shall be a dream to make our land a large home for its elders.

We invite friendship to enrich our home and we welcome beauty and kindness that our hopes may be more than a sentimental longing and that peace may abide with us.

Ernest H. Sommerfeld

POEM WRITTEN
FOR HIS WIFE GRACIE

Princess, Princess, silver maiden,
Throw your casement open; see—
 On the terrace I am singing;
Come and take the road with me!
All your gentlefolk are silken,
And your knights are stately proud—
But they do not know the hillside
 Where the daffodillies crowd,
Where the lark is mad with morning
And your heart goes mad with May,
Jesting with the wastrel breezes,
 Racing with the laughing day.

Since the morn is gray and lonely,
 Dullards call it wintertime.
But it's spring, if you are coming!
Playmate, come—or must I climb?
 (I am chilly on the terrace.
Sweetheart! Don't you hear my rhyme?)

Silver maiden, gypsy princess,
Sweetheart! Waken! It is day!
For one hour forget your duties!
For one kiss remember May!

Sinclair Lewis

The great secret of successful marriage is to treat all
disasters as incidents and none of the incidents as disasters.

Harold Nicolson

ASIDE TO HUSBANDS

What do you do when you've wedded a girl all legal
and lawful,
And she goes around saying she looks awful?
When she makes deprecatory remarks about her format,
And claims that her hair looks like a doormat?
When she swears that the complexion of which you
are so fond
Looks like the bottom of a dried-up pond?
When she for whom your affection is not the least like Plato's
Compares her waist to a badly tied sack of potatoes?
Oh, who wouldn't rather be on a flimsy bridge with
a hungry lion at one end and a hungry tiger at
the other end and hungry crocodiles underneath
Than confronted by their dearest making remarks
about her own appearance through clenched teeth?
Why won't they believe that the reason they find
themselves the mother of your children is
because you think of all the looks in the world,
their looks are the nicest?
Why must we continue to be thus constantly ordealed
and crisised?
I think it high time these hoity-toity ladies were made
to realize that when they impugn their face and
their ankles and their waist
They are thereby insultingly impugning their tasteful
husband's impeccable taste.

Ogden Nash

A man should sleep sometime between lunch and dinner in order to be at his best in the evening when he joins his wife and friends at dinner. My wife and I tried two or three times in the last forty years to have breakfast together, but it was so disagreeable we had to stop.

Winston Churchill

*Marriage is not and should not be
an interminable conversation.
The happy marriage allows for privileged silences.*

Ashley Montague

Marriage is the nursery of heaven; the virgin sends prayers to God, but she carries but one soul to him; but the state of marriage fills up the numbers of the elect, and hath in it the labour of love and the delicacies of friendship, the blessing of society and the union of hands and hearts; it hath in it less of beauty but more of safety than the single life; it hath more care, but less danger; it is more merry and more sad, is fuller of sorrows and fuller of joys; it lies under more burdens, but is supported by all the strengths of love and charity, and those burdens are delightful. Marriage is the mother of the world, and preserves kingdoms, and fills cities and churches and heaven itself.

Jeremy Taylor

THE RETURN

He has come, he is here,
My love has come home,
The minutes are lighter
Than flying foam,
The hours are like dancers
On gold-slippered feet,
The days are young runners
Naked and fleet—
For my love has returned,
He is home, he is here,
In the whole world no other
Is dear as my dear!

Sara Teasdale

A young husband and wife came to stay with us in all the first flush of married happiness. One realised all day long that other people merely made a pleasant background for their love, and that for each there was but one real figure on the scene. This was borne witness to by a whole armoury of gentle looks, swift glances, silent gestures. They were both full to the brim of a delicate laughter, of over-brimming wonder, of tranquil desire. And we all took a part in their gracious happiness. In the evening they sang and played to us, the wife being an accomplished pianist, the husband a fine singer. But though the glory of their art fell in rainbow showers on the audience, it was for each other that they sang and played. . . . These two spirits seemed, with hands intertwined, to have ascended gladly into the mountain, and to have seen a transfiguration of life: which left them not in a blissful eminence of isolation, but rather, as it were, beckoning others upwards, and saying that the road was indeed easy and plain. And so the sweet hour passed and left a fragrance behind it; whatever might befall, they had tasted of the holy wine of joy; they had blessed the cup, and bidden us, too, to set our lips to it.

A. C. Benson

Marriage is the relation between man and woman in which the independence is equal, the dependence mutual, and the obligation reciprocal.

Louis K. Anspacher

A house becomes a home through love
and respect among its residents,
not from a stylish address or a motto on the wall.

Ralph E. Howland, Jr.

We are each a secret to the other. To know one another cannot mean to know everything about each other; it means to feel mutual affection and confidence, and to believe in one another. We must not try to force our way into the personality of another. To analyze others is a rude commencement, for there is a modesty of the soul which we must recognize just as we do that of the body. No one has a right to say to another: "Because we belong to each other as we do, I have a right to know all your thoughts." Not even a mother may treat her child in that way. All demands of this sort are foolish and unwholesome. In this matter giving is the only valuable process; it is only giving that stimulates. Impart as much as you can of your spiritual being to those who are on the road with you, and accept as something precious what comes back to you from them.

Albert Schweitzer

The magic of marriage is that it creates meaningful goals to work for, struggle for, sacrifice for. It is the joint struggle that gives the relationship its meaning, and keeps people alive.

Henry Gregor Felsen

TOGETHER

You and I by this lamp with these
Few books shut out the world. Our knees
Touch almost in this little space.
But I am glad. I see your face.
The silences are long, but each
Hears the other without speech.
And in this simple scene there is
The essence of all subtleties,
The freedom from all fret and smart,
The one sure sabbath of the heart.
The world—we cannot conquer it,
Nor change the minds of fools one whit.
Here, here alone do we create
Beauty and peace inviolate;
Here night by night and hour by hour
We build a high impregnable tower
Whence may shine, now and again,
A light to light the feet of men
When they see the rays thereof:
And this is marriage, this is love.

Ludwig Lewisohn

Marriage itself is not solely an institution for the
propagation of children, but is also for the fruition of that
richer fellowship God intended when he saw that it was not
good for man to live alone.

George G. Hockman

ON MARRIAGE

You were born together, and together you shall be
forevermore.
You shall be together when the white wings of death
scatter your days.
Ay, you shall be together even in the silent memory of God.
But let there be spaces in your togetherness,
And let the winds of heaven dance between you.

Love one another, but make not a bond of love:
Let it rather be a moving sea between the shores of
your souls.
Fill each other's cup but drink not from one cup.
Give one another of your bread but eat not from the same loaf.
Sing and dance together and be joyous, but let each one of you be alone,
Even as the strings of a lute are alone though they
quiver with the same music.

Give your hearts, but not into each other's keeping.
For only the hand of Life can contain your hearts.
And stand together yet not too near together:
For the pillars of the temple stand apart,
And the oak tree and the cypress grow not in each
other's shadow.

Kahlil Gibran

Between man and wife even thoughts are contagious.

Friedrich Nietzsche

IV

BETTER THAN GOLD

It takes years to marry completely two hearts, even of the most loving and well-assorted. A happy wedlock is a long falling in love. Young persons think love belongs only to the brown-haired and crimson-cheeked. So it does for its beginning. But the golden marriage is a part of love which the Bridal day knows nothing of.

A perfect and complete marriage, where wedlock is everything you could ask and the ideal of marriage becomes actual, is not common, perhaps as rare as perfect personal beauty. Men and women are married fractionally, now a small fraction, then a large fraction. Very few are married totally, and they only after some forty or fifty years of gradual approach and experiment.

Such a large and sweet fruit is a complete marriage that it needs a long summer to ripen in, and then a long winter to mellow and season it. But a real, happy marriage of love and judgment between a noble man and woman is one of the things so very handsome that if the sun were, as the Greek poets fabled, a God, he might stop the world and hold it still now and then in order to look all day long on some example thereof, and feast his eyes on such a spectacle.

Theodore Parker

What happiness is, no person can say for another. But no one, I am convinced, can be happy who lives only for himself. The joy of living comes from immersion in something that we know to be bigger, better, more enduring and worthier than we are.

John Mason Brown

BETTER THAN GOLD

Better than gold is a peaceful home
Where all the fireside characters come,
The shrine of love, the heaven of life,
Hallowed by mother, or sister, or wife.
However humble the home may be,
Or tried with sorrow by heaven's decree,
The blessings that never were bought or sold,
And center there, are better than gold.

Abram J. Ryan

What can be more pleasant than
    to live with a wife,
matched together both in heart
    and mind,
in body and soul, sealed together
with the bond and league of a
    holy sacrament,
a sweet mate in your youth,
a thankful comfort in your age.

Erasmus

A lady of 47 who has been married 27 years and has six
children knows what love really is and once described it for
me like this: "Love is what you've been through with
somebody."

James Thurber

WEDDING ANNIVERSARY

This is the anniversary of the day
Of days, for us, when we with faith and hope
Fared forth together; solemn and yet gay
We faced the future, for life's upward slope
Was joyous going, and then we never thought
Then, that there might be worries—hours of pain
And sleepless nights that left one overwrought—
That loss would often come instead of gain.

But looking back, the time has not seemed long,
Although the road, for us, was sometimes rough . . .
We have grown quiet and the buoyant song
Once in our hearts sings low, and yet enough
Of loveliness still lives to make amend
To us, for all the ills life chose to send.

Margaret E. Bruner

Architecture has much to teach about the art of staying
married, for the basic laws of building are, likewise, the
basic laws of the home. A good foundation and balanced
proportion are essential. Honest materials are needed, for
you cannot build a noble building out of cheap, unworthy
materials and you cannot build a home to stand against the
stormy winds or worries unless you build it with the simple
virtues of faithfulness and loyalty to one another.

Robert W. Burns

He came into my life as the warm wind of spring had
awakened flowers, as the April showers awaken the earth.
My love for him was an unchanging love, high and deep,
free and faithful, strong as death. Each year I learned to love
him more and more . . .

Anna Chennault

I would like to have engraved inside every wedding band,
Be kind to one another.
This is the Golden Rule of marriage,
and the secret of making love last through the years.

Randolph Ray

I REMEMBERED

There never was a mood of mine,
Gay or heart-broken, luminous or dull,
But you could ease me of its fever
And give it back to me more beautiful.
In many another soul I broke the bread,
And drank the wine and played the happy guest,
But I was lonely, I remembered you;
The heart belongs to him who knew it best.

Sara Teasdale

HOME IS WHERE THERE'S ONE TO LOVE US

Home's not merely four square walls,
Though with pictures hung and gilded;
Home is where Affection calls,
Filled with shrines the Heart hath builded!
Home!—go watch the faithful dove,
Sailing 'neath the heaven above us;
Home is where there's one to love!
Home is where there's one to love us!

Home's not merely roof and room—
It needs something to endear it;
Home is where the heart can bloom,
Where there's some kind lip to cheer it!
What is home with none to meet,
None to welcome, none to greet us?
Home is sweet—and only sweet—
Where there's one we love to meet us!

Charles Swain

Marriage is a job. Happiness or unhappiness has nothing to do with it. There was never a marriage that could not be made a success, nor a marriage that could not have ended in bitterness and failure.

Kathleen Norris

I say, when there are spats, kiss and make up before the day is done and live to fight another day.

Randolph Ray

Success in marriage does not come merely through finding the right mate, but through being the right mate.

Barnett Brickner

The conception of two people living together for twenty-five years without having a cross word suggests a lack of spirit only to be admired in sheep.

Sir Alan Patrick Herbert

THE BOOMERANG

One unkind word in the early morn
Will poison the thoughts for the day;
One unkind look to one we love
Will take all the sunshine away.
And twice all the sunshine we take away
From the lives of others at early day
We steal from ourselves the whole day long,
And we lose the beauty of earth's glad song.

One little smile when things go wrong
Will drive off many a frown;
One pleasant look though the thoughts do rage,
Will put the tempter down.
And twice all the pleasure that we give out,
At the time when we are most tempted to pout,
Will sweeten our lives like a breath of May,
And the sun will shine through the whole glad day.

Carrie May Nichols

POEM IN PROSE

This poem is for my wife
I have made it plainly and honestly
The mark is on it
Like the burl on the knife

I have not made it for praise
She has no more need for praise
Than summer has
Or the bright days

In all that becomes a woman
Her words and her ways are beautiful
Love's lovely duty
The well-swept room

Wherever she is there is sun
And time and a sweet air
Peace is there
Work done

There are always curtains and flowers
And candles and baked bread
And a cloth spread
And a clean house

Her voice when she sings is a voice
At dawn by a freshening sea
Where the wave leaps in the
Wind and rejoices

Wherever she is it is now
It is here where the apples are
Here in the stars
In the quick hour

The greatest and richest good—
My own life to live in—
This she has given me

If giver could.

Archibald MacLeish

THERE'S MORE TO LOVE

There's more to love than loving, dear.
Though time diluting the pangs thereof,
Mellow our loving, have no fear:
There's more to love.

Some hearts are constant, others rove;
Some stake their all on now and here;
Some count in heaven their treasure-trove.
I know but this: when you are near,
Our lives are twined and tightly wove;
For, love, in you, yes, every year
There's more to love.
Paul Scott Mowrer

What greater thing is there for two human souls than to feel
that they are joined for life, to strengthen each other in all
labour, to rest on each other in all sorrow, to minister to
each other in all pain, to be one with each other in silent
unspeakable memories at the moment of the last parting?

George Eliot

Love seems swiftest, but it is the slowest of all growths. No
man or woman really knows what perfect love is until they
have been married a quarter of a century.

Mark Twain

There is nothing enduring in life for a woman except what she builds in a man's heart.

Judith Anderson

Marriage is the fusion of two hearts—the union of two lives—the coming together of two tributaries.

Peter Marshall

The kind of love that holds marriages together is not all music and sweet talk. People who feel deeply toward each other are bound to fight once in a while. The couple who brag that they have never quarreled are admitting, though they do not know it, that they simply do not care enough about each other ever to hold a frank conversation. Love is not a constant round of candy, flowers and birthday presents. It is more likely to be a long series of sacrifices in which the fishing trip gives way to a down payment on a washer and the new party dress gives way to an appendectomy and where even the weekly night out at the movies may have to give way to new shoes for the kids. It is not a guarantee of living happily ever after, for every marriage involves struggle, boredom, illness, financial problems and worry over the children. Perhaps true love can best be recognized by the fact that it thrives under circumstances which would blast anything else into small pieces.

Ernest Havemann

53

We have lived and loved together
Through many changing years;
We have shared each other's gladness
And wept each other's tears;
I have known ne'er a sorrow
That was long unsoothed by thee;
For thy smiles can make a summer
Where darkness else would be.

Like the leaves that fall around us
In autumn's fading hours,
Are the traitor's smiles, that darken
When the cloud of sorrow lowers;
And though many such we've known, love,
Too prone, alas, to range,
We both can speak of one love
Which time can never change.

We have lived and loved together
Through many changing years;
We have shared each other's gladness
And wept each other's tears.
And let us hope the future
As the past has been will be:
I will share with thee my sorrows,
And thou thy joys with me.

Charles Jefferys

Set in Palatino roman and
italic, a typeface designed
by Hermann Zapf.
Designed and illustrated by
Betsy Beach.

ACKNOWLEDGMENTS

The editor and the publisher have made every effort to trace the ownership of all copyrighted material and to secure permission from copyright holders of such material. In the event of any question arising as to the use of any material the publisher and editor, while expressing regret for inadvertent error, will be pleased to make the necessary corrections in future printings. Thanks are due to the following authors, publishers, publications and agents for permission to use the material indicated.

ABINGDON PRESS, for excerpt from *Inscape* by Ross Snyder, copyright © 1968 by Abingdon Press.

D. APPLETON-CENTURY COMPANY, INC., for excerpt from *Reason and Emotion* by John MacMurray, copyright 1938 by D. Appleton-Century Company, Inc.

ASSOCIATION FOR CHILDHOOD EDUCATION INTERNATIONAL, for excerpt by A. Powell Davies, from the September 1954 issue of *Childhood Education.*

CELESTIAL ARTS, for excerpt from *Love Is an Attitude* by Walter Rinder, copyright © 1970 by Celestial Arts Publishing.

PAUL S. ERIKSSON, INC., for excerpt from *A Thousand Springs* by Anna Chennault, copyright © 1962 by Anna Chennault.

THE GOLDEN QUILL PRESS, for "There's More to Love" from *High Mountain Road* by Paul Scott Mowrer, copyright 1962 by Paul Scott Mowrer.

GYPSY BOY MUSIC, INC., for "The Wedding Song", words and music by Buffy Sainte-Marie, copyright © 1967 by Gypsy Boy Music, Inc.

HARCOURT BRACE JOVANOVICH, INC., for "Poem Written to His Wife, Gracie" by Sinclair Lewis, from *With Love from Gracie* by Grace Hegger Lewis, copyright © 1951, 1955 by Grace Hegger Casanova; for "A Couple" from *Good Morning, America* by Carl Sandberg, copyright 1928, 1956 by Carl Sandburg.

ERNEST HAVEMANN, for excerpt from *The Intricate Balance of a Happy Marriage.*

HOLT, RINEHART AND WINSTON, for "On the Heart's Beginning to Cloud the Mind" and "The Birthplace" from *The Poetry of Robert Frost*, edited by Edward Connery Lathem, copyright 1928, © 1969 by Holt, Rinehart and Winston, copyright 1934, © 1956, © 1962 by Robert Frost.

HOUGHTON MIFFLIN COMPANY, for "The Debt" from *Door of Dreams* by Jessie B. Rittenhouse, copyright renewed 1946 by Jessie B. Rittenhouse.

ALFRED A. KNOPF, INC., for excerpt from "On Love" from *The Prophet* by Kahlil Gibran, copyright 1923 by Kahlil Gibran, renewed 1951 by Administration C.T.A. of Kahlil Gibran Estate, and Mary G. Gibran.

LITTLE, BROWN AND COMPANY, for "Word to Husbands" by Ogden Nash, copyright © 1962 by Ogden Nash; for "Aside to Husbands" by Ogden Nash, copyright 1935 by Ogden Nash.

WALTER LOWENFELS, for translation of poem, "Between Us a New Morning" by Paul Eluard.

MACMILLAN PUBLISHING COMPANY, INC., for "The Return" and "I Remembered" from *Collected Poems* of Sara Teasdale, copyright 1920 by Macmillan Publishing Company, Inc., renewed 1948 by Mamie T. Wheless.

METHUEN & CO. LTD., for "Things Lovelier" from *The Unknown Goddess* by Humbert Wolfe.

WILLIAM MORROW & COMPANY, INC., for excerpt "Why Do I Love You?" from *How to be Outrageously Successful with Women* by John Mack Carter and Lois Wyse, copyright © 1975 by John Mack Carter and Lois Wyse.

W. W. NORTON & COMPANY, INC., for excerpt from *Letters to a Young Poet* by Rainer Maria Rilke, translated by M. D. Herter Norton, copyright 1934 by W. W. Norton & Company, Inc., renewed 1962 by M. D. Herter Norton. Revised edition copyright 1954 by W. W. Norton & Company, Inc.

RANDOM HOUSE, INC., for "Poem in Prose" from *Actfive and Other Poems* by Archibald MacLeish, copyright 1948 by Archibald MacLeish.

SIMON & SCHUSTER, INC., for excerpt from *My Little Church Around the Corner* by Randolph Ray.

MAY SWENSON, for "Love Is" from *To Mix with Time* copyright © 1963 by May Swenson.

MRS. JAMES THURBER, for selection by James Thurber, copyright © 1960 by James Thurber, originally published in *Life Magazine.*